Having worked with horses, travelled extensively and run her own business, due to circumstances beyond her control J. R. Hutt was faced with a dramatic change to her lifestyle. She opted to work with disabled people which also implied a personal challenge, due to her own insecurity and anxiety in their company. However, she felt a strong desire to work closely with them and she was soon overcome by their warmth and courage. She will always be grateful to those amazing people for they taught her the power of honesty, patience, love and sheer determination.

I dedicate this book to my father, my dear friend Claire, and amazing Jan.

J. R. Hutt

STATE OF MIND

AUSTIN MACAULEY PUBLISHERS™
LONDON • CAMBRIDGE • NEW YORK • SHARJAH

Copyright © J. R. Hutt 2023

The right of J. R. Hutt to be identified as author of this work has been asserted by the author in accordance with sections 77 and 78 of the Copyright, Designs and Patents Act 1988.

All rights reserved. No part of this publication may be reproduced, stored in a retrieval system, or transmitted in any form or by any means, electronic, mechanical, photocopying, recording, or otherwise, without the prior permission of the publishers.

Any person who commits any unauthorised act in relation to this publication may be liable to criminal prosecution and civil claims for damages.

All of the events in this memoir are true to the best of author's memory. The views expressed in this memoir are solely those of the author.

A CIP catalogue record for this title is available from the British Library.

ISBN 9781398493827 (Paperback)
ISBN 9781398493834 (ePub e-book)

www.austinmacauley.com

First Published 2023
Austin Macauley Publishers Ltd®
1 Canada Square
Canary Wharf
London
E14 5AA

I would like to acknowledge all the staff and Residents at Sunnymount (which sadly is no more) where I learned so much.

My thanks to The Riding for the Disabled for all their good work.

Thanks to Christine Jones our physiotherapist for increasing my knowledge and understanding.

Thank you too to Claire whose memory and unfailing enthusiasm helped me to complete this work.

Thanks too to my husband Carlos for his support without which I could not keep writing.

Chapter 1

I was fortunate to have inherited my state of mind from my father, if indeed it is a question of genes. He was generally of a happy and positive disposition, which certainly made his life easier.

I was accordingly very content with my life. I considered myself extremely fortunate to have been born into a middle-class comfortable home and benefitted from a good education. From the middle it is possible to reach out to, and communicate with, the highest of the high and the lowest of the low in economic, educational, and social terms. Personality and mentality are quite another matter as people vary tremendously in all walks of life. There are introverts and extroverts, some are patient some very impatient, some kind some unkind, some selfish others generous, there are optimists and pessimists; the list is infinite. As I discovered to my surprise, the poor and humble can be the richest in love and generosity and some people born to wealth may be humble and kind demonstrating genuine compassion and empathy towards those less fortunate than themselves; of course, also the complete reverse can apply. I have known people who have suffered atrocities yet remain sensitive and kind whilst others are bitter and angry. There are all kinds of people from all walks of life with all kinds of mentalities, depending more on their state of mind than their actual situation. This is what makes life so fascinating; you quite simply never know what to expect – life is full of surprises! Despite the failures and problems which inevitably occur, I discovered that it is almost always true that 'Every cloud has a silver lining', although it also true that sometimes one needs to search hard and be extremely patient for it to become apparent.

A series of life's problems occurred simultaneously, as tends to happen in life, sociable things problems, they never come alone. It all began when my poor business partner developed a brain tumour. He had been a sleeping-partner, he owned the property which he rented to our business for a modest sum, and he also looked after the financial side of the business. His health deteriorated rapidly initially he began forgetting things and making mistakes which were totally out of character as he had always been extremely meticulous. Initially I was annoyed but it soon became apparent that the poor man was not well, so alas for financial and personal reasons I had to close a business which I loved.

An additional trauma being that my poor mother was having a particularly hard time. She had had all her teeth removed following repeated infections together with the teeth she completely lost her confidence. When I visited her and she covered her mouth with the sheet and refused to speak, eat, or drink with anyone present in the room. Although she was intelligent, a fighter and a worker, self-confidence had never been her strong point. Whilst still recovering and adjusting to her false teeth she had to have a hysterectomy as a tumour was detected, this in turn was followed by considerable pain and loss of mobility. The doctor told her all was well, and she should get on with her life.

Putting on a brave face she went to play tennis with friends and her hip snapped on the tennis court. We believe that when she had had a cardiac arrest following her cancer operation, they had accidentally cracked her hip during the process of reviving her. This would explain her pain and loss of mobility following the operation which was totally out of character as she was not given to complaining or giving in to pain. The hip eventually gave way on the tennis court as she only stepped backwards in a normal fashion with no brusque movement or undue exertion. However, nothing was proved, and no claims were made. As a result, my poor brave mother was in a mess.

My dear father, although he was intelligent and had a lovely disposition was not in any way, shape or form practical. Yes, he made a pot of tea every hour on the hour and spent hours in the garden, mostly smoking his pipe, or in his armchair listening to Bach or Wagner and pouring over the Financial Times, all of which frustrated Mother beyond belief. Consequently, she had been the 'jack of all trades' furthermore she was not very patient she was a veritable 'quick sticks', she was the kind of person who wanted everything done yesterday. There was nothing she wouldn't tackle, plumbing, electricity, decorating, anything that needed doing she attacked with great vigour. Meanwhile, my father stood by puffing on his pipe and marvelling at how capable she was, he always had the air of an absent-minded professor and never took offence when criticised for his incompetence.

So, with Mother out of action and Father rather lost, I returned home after an absence of over 15 years. I was not the ideal housekeeper as I had been travelling and working and never actually run a home. I remember feeling indignant towards the plants in the porch as they had made an awful mess and I had never ever seen them look so untidy, when Mother was in charge home had always been sparkling, tidy and pristine and now it was dull and untidy! When I arrived, I noticed that during the weeks while Mum had been in hospital Father had been using the same tea towel, so it looked more like a dirty floor cloth than a tea towel and there seemed to be tea stains everywhere. Father and I bumbled around and tried to get organised in time to have Mum home from hospital.

She was very agile and brilliant with her crutches she managed the stairs with no problem at all and at considerable speed. She was fiercely independent and she hated not being in-charge, so she hung a peg bag around her neck so she could carry things around the house without asking for help.

Mother improved, and Father went back to work. I finalised the closure of my business shortly afterwards my dear partner died, his family had offered to allow me to continue with the business, but I knew that it was in their best interests to sell the property, which is in fact what they did almost immediately. I attended his funeral and expressed my gratitude to the family, for his wisdom and patience during the years we had worked together. I had always been very impetuous, trying to fit a pint into a quart pot and he had invariably stopped my gallop. When I rushed into his office demanding papers and bills urgently as clients were waiting, he refused to be hurried. He would peer over his spectacles and say, "Good morning, take a seat." If I protested, he would calmly enquire, "Where is the fire?" refusing to attend to my demands until I calmed down and behaved like a reasonable human being. This was a sad ending to what had been a happy and satisfying partnership. Meanwhile I had accepted an offer of work abroad and was waiting for a work permit which was proving to be more difficult than we had anticipated.

The more my mother recovered the more redundant I became at home, although I wasn't happy about leaving her alone, so Father and I advertised for a home help. We duly interviewed Vivienne, a slight and pretty girl with a young daughter who was just starting at nursery school. We loved her from the moment we met her, she helped Mum through her difficult patch and went on to become a lifelong family friend.

Finally, I received an official letter denying me a visa and stating that they could cover the post with their own people. The position was in Quebec which was very anti English at that time. There were even factions using letter bombs and violence against the English, so maybe it was for the best. My French was fluent at the time, even so I couldn't bring myself to speak Quebecoise as they spoke French with a very strong accent interjected with a host of English vocabulary spoken with a French-Canadian accent like "le week-end".

It became increasingly apparent that I needed to look for work as poor Mother was becoming noticeably frustrated with my lack of housekeeping skills and clearly Vivienne was much better qualified in that department.

A complete career change was indicated, the world was my oyster. I had had some contact with disabled children through Riding for the Disabled and felt I would really love to work in that field. I had been terrified of physical handicap as a child as there was a girl in our guide group who had had her hand and part of her arm amputated. She always wore her sleeve rolled up and a little red stump protruding.

I was in the Brownies at the time, which I quite enjoyed but I had nightmares that when I upgraded to the Guides, we would have to dance around the campfire holding hands and I was next to this poor girl, I would wake up in a cold sweat. I also had the feeling that if I ever had to have even a finger amputated, I would literally rather die, I panicked at the thought. I refused point blank to join the guides but never told a soul the real reason.

This fear or phobia was overcome thanks to a delightful boy who had suffered when his mother took thalidomide for morning sickness. He had been born with no arms and just had three fingers protruding from his shoulders. His name was Andrew, he was 14 when I met him, had a mop of curly blond hair and lovely blue eyes and he knew I was terrified. He had amazing balance and using the invention of ladder reins manage to control his pony independently, I merely walked alongside offering occasional advice, looking into his cheeky blue eyes we chatted and joked happily enough. However, when I asked him if he needed assistance to dismount, he told me he would lean forward, then I must hold his little fingers to steady him while he swung his legs over the pony's back. I went so weak at the knees I thought I was going to pass out, but his lovely blue eyes looked steadily into mine reassuring me all would be well. As soon as I felt his warm little fingers in mine my fears of a lifetime vanished. From then onward I had no problem with physical handicap so long as I could have eye contact, I felt I could relate to, and communicate with, the person who was just like me but imprisoned in a disabled body, all thanks to dear Andrew, a lovely wise boy.

Whilst helping with the R.D.A. I also came across some mentally handicapped children. This I found more challenging, when there was little or no eye contact and communication was often bizarre, my knees would go to jelly. I was trying to help one little boy with his riding and every time I got too near to him, he tried to kick or hit me; I really didn't know how to handle the situation. I tried to help him without invading his space but felt I had failed miserably to reach him. Imagine my surprise when at the end of the class his whole expression changed, he gave me a huge smile and told me I deserved a cup of tea, he let me help him dismount and then turned and added "and a cupcake" before running off as fast as he could, the total unpredictability phased me beyond belief.

I still had hopes that the job abroad would eventually come to fruition as my would-be new employer was still in contact with me and pushing the authorities. This implied that although I wanted to work in a new sector it may only be temporary so with this in mind, I began to send off applications.

I was offered two interviews the first was as a house mother in a small home with only five young disabled children. They were heart-warmingly affectionate, their innocence and spontaneity brought tears to my eyes. How tragic for these little souls, apart from their disabilities they had no families, the home was linked to an orphanage. The lady who interviewed me was lovely, a real angel of mercy, I came away profoundly moved by the experience.

They rang me and offered me the job, but I felt that as I could not commit to long term it was not fair to these children, they needed some stability in their lives so with some sadness I turned the offer down.

The second interview was at a private home for Mentally Handicapped. The Home had been formed by a group of parents of children with Mental Handicap. This would prove to be a real challenge for me personally. As there were nearly 30 residents of all ages and disabilities, I thought there would be less danger of one-to-one dependency which was probably just a coward's way of reasoning in case I couldn't cope.

'Sunnymount' was a beautiful old house with high ceilings and lots of character it must have been an elegant family home at some point. There was a modern extension, outbuildings, garages, an extensive garden, and a paddock at the back with chicken coops and runs at the bottom of the paddock.

I was interviewed by the Administrator and the Matron, who happened to be husband and wife. Gerald was middle aged, dark-haired and stocky. I think he was of a Jewish background. He had a bit of a twinkle in his eye but had ambitious and great plans to improve the lives of his charges. Daphne was tall and well-built with short dark hair, a pretty, round face and gave the impression of being friendly, straight, efficient, and hard working. It became apparent during the interview that I had absolutely no qualifications for the job on offer.

Gerald raised his eyebrows and asked me why I thought I could do this kind of work as it is not everyone's cup of tea, he insisted on pointing out some of the more challenging aspects I would encounter. I told them I knew I wasn't qualified, but I had taught disabled children to ride and enjoyed the experience. They were waiting for more explicit details, help, so I blundered on saying I had broken-in a lot of young horses, and it requires patience and communication skills to persuade half a ton of horse to understand and do what was asked of him, plus the fact that I was keen to learn. They exchanged glances and amused smiles but offered me the job with in-house training and I was delighted.

The timetable was divided into three eight-hour shifts, everyone worked a 40hour week including one weekend in three, in addition some 'sleep-ins' being the eight hours overnight, for which this we were paid a little extra, accordingly everyone's timetable varied from week to week. All this was a short drive from my parent's house, so I would still be able to keep an eye on everything and give a hand at home, it seemed perfect and so I became an assistant housemother.

Chapter 2

On my first day I was assigned to Jayne who was a very, attractive girl with short, dark-hair, large, brown-eyes with curling lashes, and a spectacular figure. She could have been a model or a film star. She reminded me of Elizabeth Tayler however she had just been promoted to senior housemother.

The first task when coming on duty was to read the continuity book, this way we were updated, so knowing what had happened during the previous shift we knew of any changes or follow up action which may be required, and the last thing to do before going off duty was to update the continuity book with all the details of your shift.

Jayne then showed me around and it became apparent that most of the work was rather mundane, we began by dealing with the residents' clothes, there were always clean clothes to be put away, wardrobes and drawers to be sorted and tidied. There were two rather large dormitories at that time, one for girls and one for boys, then other smaller bedrooms shared by one, two or three residents.

When I arrived for my first shift most of the residents were either at Special School or the older ones at a Training Centre. A few stayed at home because they didn't feel well, and some always stayed at home to help in the house or work in the garden and grounds so it was a gentle introduction.

The daily staff consisted of a gardener, a cook, cleaning staff, Madge the laundress, Anne the seamstress and Jill the Secretary, all of whom I got to know over lunch, then there was the care staff who I met little by little as they all worked different shifts.

Jayne and I were in the boy's dormitory when the coach arrived bringing some of the residents' home and there was a noisy avalanche as they burst through the front door, subsequently half a dozen lads charged into the dormitory, most rushed to put their things away but Andree stood transfixed with his mouth open his eyes raised to heaven pointing at me spluttering over and over again, "A new one!" Then he rushed towards me flinging his arms around me. I lost balance and fell backwards fortunately onto a bed with Andree on top of me. He was only 12 years old but a stocky boy with Down syndrome, (or trisomy 21 as the condition is sometimes called because it is due to all, or part of a third copy of chromosome 21). People with Down syndrome often have stinted physical development, although they tend to put on weight. They have a characteristic round face with small eyes, and they rarely develop mentally beyond the age of an eight or nine years old, although all of this varies with each case. Andree was taller than most, with spikey fair hair and he was considerably heavier and certainly stronger than me. Fortunately, Jayne came to the rescue. "Andree!" she screamed. "Get up, and put her down you don't know where she has been! What is more she won't come again if you treat her like that!" With this Andree sheepishly extricated himself grinning and giggling, then Jayne introduced me to them all, one by one. They all reacted differently, and it was not easy to decipher what some of them were feeling or thinking. Some were excited like Andree, some reticent and shy and others totally indifferent. Mick rolled his eyes to heaven and never looked directly at you, which fazed me a bit, he was brain damaged and although he was old and gruff, he proved to be a gentle giant.

Andree was a happy soul, rather hyperactive and a bubbly extrovert. When things calmed down, he sought me out and to my amazement inquired, "Parlez vous francaise mademoiselle?" to which I replied, "Bien sur monsieur, et toi aussi?" following which we launched into a conversation in French. He was not only fluent but had an excellent accent. I was astounded to say the least.

Andree's father was French, and Andree went to France for a holiday with his father for two weeks every year. How strange is the mind, a boy who had difficulty tying his shoelaces was completely bi-lingual, although he had frankly terrified me at our first meeting, I became extremely fond of Andree, he was boisterous and with a tendency to play tricks, but he loved to practice his French and was always happy and full of fun.

I was to discover that despite their problems, in some ways, many of them had extraordinary talents, gifts or knowledge. I will mention just a few who impressed me in this way.

Katy was brain damaged from birth and she had epileptic seizures with certain frequency, (this was caused by a burst of electrical activity in the brain affecting oral activity). Sometimes she just lost awareness and stared blankly into space but frequently she had fits when she would go stiff, and her body would go into spasm and jerk uncontrollably. When this happened, we held her head to one side to keep her airway clear, loosened any tight clothing and gave her space trying not to restrict her movements too much. Poor Katy she was very highly strung, she was hyperactive and often knew when she was about to have a fit, sometimes she had a tingling feeling or strange sensations of smell or taste and would call out to us repeatedly, "She is going to have a fit!" whilst running around in a frenzy poor girl. She was on a considerable amount of medication but if seizures are caused by stress she seemed permanently stressed and easily upset which didn't help her.

However, she was fascinated with figures and loved mathematics she was constantly rushing around 'doing sums' as she put it. I shared her love of mathematics and was happy to spend time with her doing simple arithmetic and developing her skills. It seemed so sad if she hadn't been brain-damaged she would probably have gone far. She was very quick to learn and rushed around talking incessantly, she was 12 years old and added to her problems had just started her period which rather frightened her plus she had awful acne. She had antibiotics and her skin improved a little but the acne had caused some scarring, she was also put on the pill, partly as a precaution and partly to control her periods, poor child.

Social life and volunteers were encouraged and there was an outing to a Pantomime.

My friend Carlos volunteered to come and help. I was sitting next to Katy and the music and bright lights excited her to the point that she went into seizure, I pulled her across my lap in order to turn her head and she kicked and launched herself across to Carlos so he took charge of her head and I tried to avoid her kicking the people beside and in front of us, but without restricting her too much, not easy in that situation, it lasted only a couple of minutes but seemed like a lifetime, following which poor Katy was then drowsy for the rest of the show which was probably a blessing as the lights and music had over stimulated her.

John was the same age as Katy and like her brain damaged from birth, but he was totally different from Katy, despite this they went to school together and were inseparable friends. John was a thin, shy and rather nervous boy, he was not very articulate but as Katy never stopped talking the friendship worked well, what is more he seemed devoted to her.

Another, a really, surprising case was Hilary who was also brain damaged from birth. Hilary was about 30 years old, tiny in stature if a little plump, she had very thin fair hair and blue eyes, she was usually looking down, wringing her hands, sometimes biting her knuckles, and almost always muttering to herself. It was almost impossible to have a coherent conversation with her, and not easy to coax her into doing anything if she thought otherwise, be it coming to the dining room or going to bed. When out walking she would suddenly crouch down, this could happen anywhere, on the pavement, in a shop or in the middle of the road, she would then cover her head with her hands and scream, "Leave her! Leave her!" repeatedly as if someone were attacking her. If you approached her to try to calm her or persuade her to move, she would add your name to the screams. Hilary was quite a challenge, and we got some very funny looks from members of the public, fortunately most of the local community knew her.

I had a little dog at that time, and I was encouraged to take her to work as many of the residents related well towards animals. The first time my little dog went into the lounge where Hilary was, Hilary looked up immediately pointed at "Fleur", my little dog, and shouted out very clearly, "Jack Russel Terrier!" Amazing, we later discovered her mother had had a Jack Russel when she was a child.

Hilary surprised us in other aspects too. I was having singing lessons and studying the theory of music at the time, an aspect of my education which had been sadly neglected. When I was alone with my group of residents, I would sometimes play some classical music. On one such evening I put on some music and Hilary jumped to her feet. "Beethoven's Symphony number 6 Pastoral," she shouted. She was spot on and proved to have a far wider knowledge of classical music than I ever aspired to, she recognised nearly every piece I played, apparently her mother had played a lot of classical music when she was small. She was quite knowledgeable yet incapable of holding a normal conversation.

Hilary also related to animals, as I mentioned previously, she had recognised my little dog and loved her. At one point we had a goat in the paddock which had kids and we made them a cosy stable in one of the garages. Hilary was besotted with them, she often escaped, and we found her crouched down talking to the baby goats. Although it was sometimes hard to get her to leave them to come in for her tea it proved an asset when we were out, when she went into her crouch down and shout mode, we simply said, "Come on Hilary, let's go and see the baby goats." She would calm down, stop shouting and happily cooperate.

Sally was completely different, she was in her twenties and in many ways very a very capable girl although she still wet the bed almost every night, she would strip the bed herself and take the sheets down to the laundry muttering to herself. However, she loved sewing and her hand sewing was identical to that of machine sewing. She sewed with tiny, neat stitches that were completely even and straight, quite perfect, and beautiful the only downside being if they needed unpicking, they were so tiny and tight, it was quite a challenge. Sally was tireless she would stitch away for hours and loved to sit and sew with Anne the seamstress.

Then there was dear Tommy who was one of the older residents he was tall and thin and going bald. Tommy was probably Autistic, he spoke very, little, the occasional word or short phrase with a lot of stammering so he had difficulty communicating. Tommy was mostly happy but especially so when tending the plants and animals although when nervous he would giggle, fidget, and scratch his head. He worked at home and was in-charge of the chickens under the supervision of the Gardener. He took great care when collecting the eggs and I am sure he talked to the chickens more than to us.

Tommy was a sad case as he had been abandoned as a baby. Even sadder he was left on the steps of a Mental Hospital which had since been closed, so he had been brought up in a Mental Institution which must have been a strange environment for a child to grow up in. When the Hospital was closed the Authorities moved him to 'Sunnymount'. He had settled in very well considering his background and he was a great asset working in the garden as well as with the chickens and sheep.

Peter worked with Tommy although they were as different as chalk from cheese. Pete was Down syndrome, he was a hard-working lad, reliable and capable, he was short and wiry with a mop of spiky dark hair, and he was very affectionate. Peter worked with Tommy in the garden and helped with the chickens, he would also sometimes help in the kitchen. He never complained and would wash up all day if you let him.

Edna was very friendly with Tommy and Peter and she worked in the house, she was the oldest resident, a simple soul but did not seem to be disabled as such. She had had three children which had sadly been taken from her by social services and they didn't know where to send her, so she ended up at 'Sunnymount'. Fortunately, she seemed happy with the arrangement and took on a mothering role with some of the residents. Her life must have been extremely hard who knows what really happened to her. When talking to her she always emphasised that the Social Worker said she kept everywhere nice and clean, but she rarely talked about the children and as far as I knew no one ever visited her.

Johnny and Michael were two lads with Down syndrome, they were similar in appearance although not related but they were firm friends. They were both short in stature and rather overweight but very affectionate and with a great sense of humour although sometimes they could be stubborn. Johnny was especially friendly with Annie who was also Down syndrome and with Mary who was older and very fond of Johnny. Sometimes they would refuse to do something, for example go to bed or get dressed, they might sit on the floor like a two-year-old having a tantrum, the difference being that you can pick a two-year-old up and take them to bed, not so with a nine or ten stone Down syndrome boy. As a result, it took a lot of patience and psychology to persuade them to do something if they were not inclined to cooperate, having said that they were extremely affectionate and loving. They all related to some members of staff better than others, just depending on the chemistry I suppose as we all did our best but with varying results.

On the other hand, Geoffrey who was also downs syndrome was taller, not overweight and had very dark hair and eyes, he stuttered and was not very articulate but was a very gentle soul and he was wonderful at cleaning shoes. We sometimes had a little shoe cleaning group and would spread a huge sheet on the floor and sit in a circle, it was a bit messy sometimes, the polish seemed to get everywhere, but Geoffrey would take a shoe and brush it and brush it until it shone like glass, you just had to remind him to turn the shoe around now and again to polish the other side, the front or the back. He would sit happily polishing long after the others had finished and put their shoes away.

My heart went out to Angela, a young girl with bright red hair, and she was also blind. She was very gentle but had a habit of rocking incessantly which is also a sign of mental illness. Rocking does trigger the brain to release endorphins in the body which make you feel good, (the word endorphin comes from endogenous meaning 'in the body' and 'morphine' which alleviates pain). Thinking about it we rock babies to sooth them to sleep and in the past elderly people or nursing mothers had rocking chairs, so it makes sense that rocking is comforting. However, sometimes Angela's rocking was exaggerated to the point she could harm herself or lose her balance.

Then there was Tracy the youngest resident, and she was also blind, she had learned to use a stick to give her more independence. It is hard when these poor souls have multiple handicaps to deal with, as with Gerald who was a Down syndrome boy with the added difficulty of a cleft palate. This made eating uncomfortable although it in no way diminished his appetite, he loved his food, it also affected his speech and although he tried to communicate, he was not always easy to understand and at times he was understandably frustrated. When we later had a pony, he was passionate about her and when he couldn't be found he was invariably in the paddock talking to Peggy the pony and he grew to love his riding. Peggy of course, always understood what he was trying to say, and she never contradicted him!

There was also hyperactive young David who had Down syndrome, a thin, blond, boy, and tall brain damaged David who rolled his head and his eyes but was a quiet and gentle. These were but a few, each resident had their distinctive personality and their individual problems to overcome. What was most surprising was their spontaneity and capacity for love, their innocence being like that of a young child, although this rather sadly also made them extremely vulnerable.

Chapter 3

Claire was the deputy Matron, she was a qualified social worker who clearly had a calling for helping those in need, and fighting vehemently for anyone who was underprivileged. She had fair, curly hair and blue eyes and with her gentle Irish brogue and the first impression she gave was of anything but the fiery and passionate girl she proved to be. Claire had recently married and was a strict vegetarian, so she fretted over the Residents' diet. Daphne's family had run a fish and chip shop, so chips and fried food were often on the menu. Claire was violently opposed to fried food and strangely to onions which she said were very harsh, it is true that they can cause gases and bloating, also skin irritation not to mention weepy eyes. However, onions can also lower cholesterol and help to maintain blood pressure and weight, which for our Downs friends could be helpful. There is an old-wives' tale which states that if you put onions in your socks, you can kill a flu virus!

Gerald and Daphne had previously run a care home for the elderly and Daphne confessed she loved working with old people. At the time they lived, with their two young sons, in a two bedroomed flat, above the games room which was in a separate building. However, they were in the process of buying a house in the town only a short distance away. Tommy and Peter helped them considerably with the preparation and the move and they eventually moved out thus leaving the two-bedroom apartment vacant.

Maggie was the Assistant Matron, she was young, energetic, practical, and hard-working, I believe her parents also ran a Care Home for the Elderly, so she had background experience of running a Residential Home. As now empty flat was two bedroomed the chance came up for two of us to move in, as no one else was interested I jumped at the opportunity. Things were fine at home but having been away for so long as Mother recovered it was rather like being a child again. Little things, for example as I was going out Mum would demand, "Where are you going in those shoes? Don't you know it is pouring with rain?" So, to avoid argument I would change into my boots, and as I left the house Father would say, "Why are you wearing boots; it isn't winter?" It was funny really but then in my thirties having travelled the world and run my own business I found it a bit wearing.

Fleur, my little dog, and I moved into 'Sunnymount' where I also had a garage for the car. Maggie and I were to share, she was easy to live with, she was neat and tidy and as we worked alternate shifts we did not often coincide, but we took it in turns to clean, she always cleaned the fridge, and I cleaned the cooker, it worked fine.

Maggie loved curry and often ordered a take-away. She also loved a drink; she drank gallons of lager which occasionally got her into trouble. I had a Spanish friend called Carlos, and when he came back from Spain, he brought a suitcase full of Larios Gin which was made in his hometown of Malaga. One evening he rang to say he had just arrived back from Malaga, and could he come around, I was on duty until 10 pm but that was fine because Maggie was in the flat and quite happy to entertain him until I came off duty. When I finished work, I found the two of them as 'Happy as Larry' they had drunk a whole bottle of gin between them! Carlos said not to worry he had another bottle which we could take around to his friend David!

On another occasion Gerald had a formal dinner to attend and Daphne was not well so he took Maggie, she wore a long dress and really looked stunning, however, I was awoken by loud voices at about 2 am I found Gerald and Maggie arguing at the bottom of the stairs. Gerald just said that she had had too much to drink as usual. I helped Maggie upstairs and put her to bed, but she was sobbing uncontrollably which was not the usual effect drink had on her.

Gerald was a bit of a lad, on Valentine's Day I received a home-made card, I assumed it was from one of the residents but couldn't ascertain who was responsible. I had been asking around if anyone knew who had sent it when Gerald appeared and called me to his office, he told me to take a seat, then looking down and fiddling with his pen he said, "Actually I sent you the valentine and I mean every word of it." That took the wind out of my sails. Then a wave of anger swept over me, he had a wife and two children all of whom I saw every single day, how could he be so brazen. Admittedly I am a bit of a prude, and I was rather cruel, I laughed in his face and refused to take him seriously. Following that interview he was always correct but decidedly distant which suited me fine. The whole situation was bizarre as he was supposedly devoutly religious and upright. Sadly, some years later he and Daphne split up, it must have been devastating for Daphne who was a good sort and a great mother, fortunately her sons stood by her. Gerald was a social climber and a bit of a charmer and because I was uncomfortable with this side of his character, I probably didn't appreciate all he had achieved, which with hindsight had been innovative and creative. Being a social climber, he became buddies with the mayor, other local dignitaries and wealthy businessmen as a result of which he was able to make a lot of improvements so enhancing the lives of the residents in many ways.

Debbie was a vibrant, spontaneous young girl with a mop of slightly ginger, fair, curly, hair; she was a bit wild but had a big heart.

Debbie also had tolerance and empathy with situations I found hard to deal with. Tuesday and Thursday were bath nights, there were half a dozen bath rooms and the girls bathed one night and the boys another. We would run all the baths and supervise them undressing and getting in, some were more independent and others needed total supervision, sometimes the warm water would encourage them to open their bowels, the first time I found faeces floating around a boy in the bath I didn't know how to react, but Debbie reacted calmly and naturally helping the boy out of the bath, wrapping him in a towel, cleaning up and running him a fresh bath, she explained they don't have the concepts and inhibitions we have and it is just a natural process provoked by the relaxing in the warm water. There was one girl in particular who would masturbate anywhere, again I was dumbfounded and nonplussed as to how to deal with the situation, but Debbie simply put her arm around the girl saying, "Come on, love, you'll be much more comfortable in your bedroom," so leading her in the right direction without any aggravation.

Jayne and Debbie also lived in and shared a bedsit in the main house. They both had boyfriends at the time and apparently Debbie had had a tiff with her boyfriend and was extremely upset. I was on duty at the time and vaguely aware of the situation, but Debbie was off duty. Suddenly there was incessant ringing of the front-door bell and when I answered it was Debbie's mother, she was bordering on complete hysteria. "Where is my daughter!!!" she screamed at me. I replied in as calm a voice as I could muster, "She is not on duty, so I don't know, try her room." At this point, her mother launched herself into the hall and attacked me with "You jolly well should know, she is upset, and she has taken off in the car. I knew you wouldn't look after her here!!!"

I recovered my composure after this onslaught and perhaps a little unkindly retaliated, "My job is to look after the residents, and if the staff can't even look after themselves it is a poor show; their private life is not my responsibility!" Of course, I would have helped Debbie if I had been able to, but I was indignant at this verbal onslaught by a mother who was beside herself. However, we sat her down and gave her a cup of tea and she regained her composure, fortunately Jayne was able to throw some light on the matter as to Debbie's whereabouts, so she left somewhat placated.

Ingrid was practical, down-to-earth and good fun. She had a mass of tight curly, fair hair and lived on a narrow boat with her boyfriend. The canal ran alongside the Home, so she only had to walk about a hundred yards to get to work, she was an assistant housemother like me, she was very down to earth, practical and a had abundant common sense, she got on well with both staff and residents.

There was also a tall thin lad who joined the team, Pete, who was great with the lads, and it was also good to have some strong muscles to hand plus he was popular with both staff and residents and very much in demand.

Another male member of the care team joined us, David was quiet and caring, he was dark and gentle I really liked the way he related to the quieter more retiring residents there was an air of calm about him. However, when he and I took a small group of residents on holiday we all stayed in a caravan and one night I was awoken by a rumpus and he was having a seizure, quite a strong one at that. The next day he seemed exhausted, I asked him if he had told our employers about his epilepsy, he hadn't, he said he was sure he wouldn't have got the job if he had. I told him it was a mistake because there could have been an accident and I was sure they would understand, and perhaps for example he shouldn't do sleep-ins alone. I hoped they would sort it out and give him an opportunity as he was so good with the residents, an asset to the team and a lovely person. We continued our holiday with our little group with no more incidents he was kind, good fun and excellent at his job.

One of the good things about 'Sunnymount' was that it was divided into family groups, there were mixed ages and disabilities so bonding, and relationships formed in a natural way. The residents spontaneously helped each other within their limitations and they also assisted us with small tasks according to their abilities, as would happen in any family.

Gerald the administrator was also the resident chiropodist and treated all the residents plus he had other private clients. Due to his workload, he found it a bit much and at one staff meeting he enquired if anyone would be interested in taking over his part time practice, this would involve studying with the SMAE Institute by correspondence, doing the practical work alongside Gerald and buying his equipment little by little. No one seemed interested so I volunteered to give it a go.

Some people have an aversion to feet (including my mother), and most of us tend to neglect them (including myself) until they cause a problem. I had never given them much consideration, yet they are essential for our mobility.

Treating the residents proved to be a good training ground, there were all kinds of feet, club foot, web toes, hallux valgus (bunions), hammer toes, not to mention verrucas, corns, ingrown toenails, etc. Added to this was the psychological challenge of persuading some of the residents to even allow you to cut their toenails.

The biggest challenge was Annie, Gerald said it would be a miracle if she ever let anyone cut her toenails without a fight, he was big and strong, and they got on the floor then he held her foot leaning against her to immobilise her and neatly cut her nails ignoring her desperate wailing! I would never be able to do that, nor did I want to try, but I loved a challenge so every time I was on duty, I asked Annie to show me her toes. I confess I sometimes bribed her with a sweet, she would take off her sock and shoe and hold her foot in front of me, but if I went too near, she would swing away shaking her head with a vehement "NO!!!" After weeks of patience, she would hold her toe and let me cut the nail, but she never let me hold her foot. At least I kept her nails down without a fight and I encouraged her to file them herself with an emery board.

The staff had regular training days, talks on general subjects like hygiene, nutrition and first aid, and through our daily work we encountered doctors, psychologists and physiotherapists, people from special education and training, volunteers, fund raisers, a wide range of professionals and generally both interesting and caring people.

A few of the residents had visitors from family members but all too few. Having a disabled child can be very enriching but also very demanding and life changing for the whole family. Statistics show there are fewer divorces in families where there is a disabled child, difficulties either make or break relationships. Sadly, as had happened with many of our residents, they had been cared for at home until the parents were too old to cope physically or they passed away, so their offspring suddenly found themselves in a residential home or an institution and a completely different environment. It was understandably hard for them to adapt. Robert a red headed lad was one such case, he had lived in a nearby village where everyone knew him. He still had visits from his Auntie, and he occasionally visited her, but she was not young enough to cope with him at home.

In the past Down syndrome children rarely lived beyond their teens as there was a risk of congenital heart defects, autism, and seizures among other things. They also tend to have weak chests, and many died of pneumonia. Some people blamed institutionalisation for their shortened lives. Thanks to modern medicine today they are rushed to hospital and treated with massive doses of antibiotics so mostly recover. They also have a better lifestyle and can live up to 60 years old, but this means their parents die before them or can no longer cope which is heart-breaking for everyone.

I remember one night when I was sleeping in, Andree woke up with a raging temperature, I rang Maggie who was on call, and she told me to call an ambulance immediately. Andree was rushed into hospital, sure enough he had pneumonia and they were swift to treat him. We were all so relieved when he recovered and returned home. We have the same dilemma now with the elderly, if we can help someone to live longer, we will, it is instinctive to save loved ones and prolong life. However, sometimes this leads to poor quality of life and prolonged suffering, we need to question our true motives is it to satisfy our own conscience, or keep the person with us at all costs, or really for the benefit of the person, these are very tricky ethical questions we need to ask ourselves. Part of our human mindset is 'where there is life there is hope' and it can lead to incredible, even miraculous recovery, it is a powerful one but can be either wonderful or heart-breaking.

Chapter 4

One of Gerald's brainwaves was to make an appeal on Television to form a group of volunteers. For some reason he asked me to make the appeal, probably due to the fact my mother had sent me for elocution lessons when I was young, plus the fact I had lived in so many different places, as a result I had no strong accent, more of a BBC accent. Times have changed but at that time everyone on the Television had the same accent, a BBC accent and mine fitted the bill. I had also lost any trace of my Birmingham accent from travelling around so much added to which I had done quite a lot of public speaking and acting which helped considerably.

I went to the Television studio and was sent to the dressing room where a lady set about applying make-up in copious quantities. I pleaded with her to make it as light as possible, but she layered it on 'with a trowel', as my mother would have said, to the point where I felt I was wearing a mask and if I tried to speak it would crack! I am not sure what she did with my hair but that felt odd too, it was rather like being dressed up as the wicked stepmother to go on stage!

I was ushered through to the studio and seated before the cameras, the make-up lady still fluttering around with the powder puff as the lights came up, evidently, I still didn't look the part.

I was not discouraged in fact I was quite confident as I had prepared my speech well. My father had been famous for his speeches and was always being invited to speak at both social and business events, I remember him preparing at home and using me as a guinea pig audience, and I have since prepared many foreign businesspeople, helping them to give presentations in English. I knew the drill, not too long or people switch off, timing to present the punch lines when people have settled down and before they lose interest or go to sleep. I had learned techniques to recapture your audience if you think they are not paying full attention and above all to be passionate about your topic. Following in my father's footsteps I had prepared well, but found it rather cold talking to a camera lens, I preferred talking to real people. It was easy as my text was written up in huge letters just below the camera. As a result, I was mortified when the director kept stopping me and it took about four takes to complete the appeal.

When I got back to 'Sunnymount' I was rushed in before I could scrape the make-up off my face. Everyone without exception said what a vast improvement and the makeup lady had worked wonders, they all approved of my new look. I laughed and told them I was sorry, but no way was I going to spend precious hours of the day on my appearance, they would have to put up with my previous, natural look.

The campaign proved to be a huge success we were inundated with calls. Soon the first meeting for 'Friends of Sunnymount' was arranged. It was held in the evening in the Games Room. Gerald gave an introductory speech about the home, the residents, and possible objectives for the future. Then a committee was formed following introductions and ideas put forward. They were a lovely bunch of people and very enthusiastic.

Fund raising ideas came forward and it was obviously going to be a great social group too. The idea was to raise funds for holidays, activities, facilities, and equipment to benefit the lives of the residents.

A proposal which I had put forward in the campaign was then put into action. The idea was for normal families to adopt a resident who had no family of their own, and to take them out once a week if possible. A charming man came up to me afterwards and asked me who was the most, needy, resident, I had no hesitation, our cuddly, affectionate Down children were very appealing and popular, I suggested Tommy, I explained he was an ageing, autistic man who had been brought up in a Mental Hospital and had no family. Dan didn't hesitate, he was a family man with a wife and two children, and he arranged for the family to come and meet Tommy.

We dressed Tommy up in a jacket and tie and explained he would be having a special visitor; he was nervous and excited. The family arrived, a delightful family with two children who were about eight and ten years old, we ushered them into the lounge and served tea to them all with Tommy who was grinning from ear to ear. Later Tommy took them down the paddock to show them the chickens and around the garden gesticulating to show them that he had weeded one bed and the plants he had planted. Following this they came every Sunday after lunch and took him home to tea. Tommy visibly blossomed, he was noticeably happier, and his communication improved. On Sundays he would get all dressed up in the morning, having badgered Pete into shaving him properly, then he would pace up and down in front of the window saying to anyone who would listen, "Don, Don coming!" all the time pointing proudly from his chest to the front gates. If only someone had adopted dear Tommy when he was young his life could have been so different.

The 'Friends' did great work organising events, developing special relationships with residents, and raising money, they became part of the 'Sunnymount' family.

On Sunday there was a small group of residents who wanted to go to church. Whenever I was on duty on Sunday, I took them down to evensong at the local church; a short walk from the home. They loved it and sang with great gusto, even if it was off key, they had no inhibitions. The vicar was a kindly soul who took the trouble to talk to us after the service. He asked me if any of them had been confirmed, not surprisingly none of them had. They all showed great enthusiasm although I wasn't sure if they fully understood what it entailed. The vicar asked me if I would like to bring the group to confirmation classes, they were so excited, how could I refuse, so I promised to consult the management. Gerald was always open to new ideas especially when it involved introducing our charges into the community in normal social activities, so he gave us the green light.

The little group consisted of Tommy, Peter, Johnny, Michael and Mary and Sally, they were all mature in age but they were very keen and so we started to attend the communion classes. We joined a group of young people who all showed kindness and consideration, such young folk restore one's faith in humanity. I had been confirmed in the same church many years previously although of late my contact with the church had been scant. It is hard to know how much of what the vicar said my charges really understood, but their state of mind and attitude had a purity and an innocence in their total acceptance of everything, that I am sure God would have approved. They loved the bible stories and those who were able to, enjoyed telling the other residents what they had learned, never questioning, or doubting for a moment. I thought not for the first time we could learn a lot from their example. Somewhere there is a balance between questioning everything and blindly accepting everything, the trouble is finding it!

The day of their confirmation there was great excitement, Edna was very emotional and kept weeping and wrapping her arms tightly around my waist, hugging me and thanking me between sobs. They were all dressed up in their best clothes and a large group of staff and residents came to support them. We had had a rehearsal in the church the day before, but I must admit I was nervous too.

They were being confirmed with the rest of the group, all youngsters, and the church would be full. This was true integration into a community and fortunately all went smoothly. We went to the vicarage afterwards for refreshments where they mingled and talked to people from the parish, people who not only accepted but admired them. All thanks to a vicar who was open and generous, he will never know how much it meant to them and indeed to us.

The first holiday I went on with the home was to Pontins. I had never been to a holiday camp and to be honest I was not particularly looking forward to it. Preparing the suitcases was quite a marathon, preceded by individual shopping trips, for example many of the residents had never had swimwear.

There was a buzz of excitement running through the home during the weeks preceding the holiday.

Finally, the day came, a coach came to collect us, and we took out the luggage then piled on board. It was a jovial trip; there was a lot of banter, singing and merriment.

The apartments slept six; they were in single story, prefabricated chalets, or bungalow like buildings. We split up each member of staff with their assigned group of residents. On entering our allotted apartment, I found it a little dark and musty, but my little group were not daunted so we settled in and unpacked amid a great furore of anticipation. There was a small bathroom and a tiny kitchenette where we could make drinks and snacks.

We had arranged a meeting point after meals, to which we would take our little groups individually. There were activities organised all day every day and this I must admit was popular with our charges. The mental age of most of our residents was way below their actual age so they were often taking part in activities with smaller children, mostly the children were lovely with them, children tend not to judge in the same way as adults, so our charges had a really good time. In the evenings there was music, dancing and entertainment also interspersed with talent shows, dancing competitions, comedians, quizzes and other activities, the staff worked hard.

On the last evening there was a Beauty Contest, our residents were urging us to take part. After much badgering I reluctantly took to the catwalk doing my best not to fall flat on my face. I had my little fan club whooping and cheering and to my utter surprise I came second!

I took my little group to the beach when I could although the weather was not ideal and the beach rather dull and deserted, however we collected shells and pebbles and I encouraged them to paddle, it was good for us all to smell the sea air again.

The food was a little too abundant in both quantity and calories for our friends, who had insatiable appetites and a tendency to put on weight, but it was only temporary, and they enjoyed themselves tremendously, so despite my reservations, overall, I have to admit it was a successful venture.

There was great elation the day the Minibus arrived. Gerald drove it initially and then at a staff meeting he asked if anyone else would like to drive it. I volunteered as I had driven all kinds of vehicles from tractors, Land Rovers, cars with trailers, small horseboxes under three tons, sports cars, and anything else on wheels.

Gerald had a brainwave; to test our driving skills, he parked the minibus in the entrance facing the road and the first time we drove it we had to reverse, using mirrors only, down the narrow drive which curved around the house and past all the outbuildings to the car park at the rear. I was lucky having had plenty of experience; once I was driving a car and trailer with two horses on board and I went the wrong way down a one-way street in the middle of Geneva. I came face to face with an irate driver and had to reverse the trailer all the way back down the street under the duress of an irate man relentlessly sounding his horn and shaking his fist at me, so the minibus test was no sweat in comparison. All said and done, in retrospect it was still a brave thing for Gerald to have done, we could easily have scraped the shiny new vehicle on the corner wall of the house or scratched it on the bushes, however, his judgement proved good and the minibus survived intact. Having our own minibus opened up all kinds of possibilities to take groups of residents on outings of all kinds so widening their horizons. This also changed the plans for the summer holidays; instead of going on mass to a holiday camp it enabled us to take small groups on caravan holidays to the country or near the sea.

My first long trip driving the minibus was to the Lake District and we set off with great anticipation, the minibus was comfortable and easy to drive, and we had a spacious caravan waiting for us on the edge of the National Park. We sang most of the way only stopping off for a picnic and to enjoy the glorious sunshine which we hoped would last for at least a few more days, only too aware that the beautiful Lakes were renowned for their abundant rainfall. However, it would take more than rain to dampen our spirits.

The caravan park was in a lovely setting with beautiful green countryside and magnificent views all around, enhanced of course by the glorious sunshine. We unpacked and settled in then set off to find the shops and stock up on food. Our charges loved being involved with a simple activity like going food shopping and we learned, sometimes to our surprise, what they liked and disliked. Living in a residence, with all the will in the world, they had a limited choice as to what to eat and drink and when they saw the variety of goodies in the supermarket their little eyes goggled. Equally the novelty of choosing and preparing their own meals, then washing up afterwards was a new experience for some of them. It was so beneficial being in a small group, for all of us.

The personal closeness in those beautiful surroundings seemed to soothe both emotional and physical problems. We made our plans for the following day as a family group trying to include activities to suit everyone. Walking was not easy for everyone so some days we split up for half a day to allow the more physically active to enjoy the lovely walks. If there wasn't anything nearby for the less active simply being in the countryside making daisy chains, dabbling toes in a babbling brook, listening to the birds or drawing wildflowers was a welcome change from routine.

We wanted to show them the famous peaks and lakes but sometimes trying to take the less mobile of our group as high as possible proved a little risky. I confess that I was a little anxious on more than one occasion when climbing a narrow, winding, one way track-like road with nowhere to pass and nowhere to turn, fortunately the minibus didn't let us down and I learned to ask the locals before embarking on mountain climbing adventures with the minibus full of children! They learned to recognise Scafell Pike one of the horse-shoe, and the highest peak in England standing over 3,000 feet above sea level. When I saw there was a car park at Lake Head, I thought it would be fine, but even that was nearly eight kilometres of single-track road. There were easier and beautiful walks around the lakes near Ambleside and Keswick with access to pubs and shops. The more active members of our group managed the Catbells walk near Keswick, a beginners' walk truly underestimated as it has spectacular views of Derwentwater, Castlerigg Fell and Borrowdale with plenty of easy parking in lay-bys.

There were lovely picnic spots too like Gummer's How and Buttermere, but it took us half the morning to prepare the picnic as everyone wanted to help and make sure we included their favourite goodies.

There were plenty of other things to do, a "must" for me being The World of Beatrix Potter in Bowness-on-

Windemere with its delightful Peter Rabbit Garden reflecting, details of the stories and adventures of Peter Rabbit like the watering can where he hid and the blue jacket which he had lost adorning the scarecrow. Hilary and Katy loved it too and we truly indulged, although the boys would probably have preferred to play football! The World of Beatrix Potter apart from being delightful is also educational caring for the environment, all in keeping with Beatrix Potter's passion as she was a pioneer of conservation, she loved nature and had generously donated an extensive amount of land to the National Trust enabling us all to still enjoy it today.

There were four steam train rides, round lakes through woodland and with sea views, plus the quarry and mining museum, so plenty to choose from and something for everyone to enjoy. It was also possible to hire a boat although no one seemed too keen on the idea.

We had a thoroughly enjoyable week mostly managing to dodge the showers. One day in swimwear and the next in wellies, according to the changeable climate which in some way added to the variety and sense of fun usually causing giggles and disbelief!

The Variety Club did great work raising money for handicapped children and they organised a rally and fancy-dress competition in London. The fancy dress was also for the minibuses! We spent weeks preparing and involved everyone, by popular vote the theme chosen was Clowns, so how do you dress up a minibus as a clown? We made masses of papier mache a bath full in fact, that was great fun, we made a huge nose and a great pointed hat which when dry we painted in the garden, so everyone had a go! Then we made masses of flowers out of crepe paper and great ruffles all very brightly coloured. We had even greater fun dressing up a group of residents as clowns with the help of Anne the seamstress and Sally who stitched tirelessly all day every day to her hearts content. Finally, off we went to London, fortunately it didn't rain and it was truly spectacular, hundreds of minibuses all dressed up, I can't remember who won but it was not important it proved a great day out we met so many like-minded people from all over the country!

The following summer we held a huge garden party to celebrate the Royal Wedding between Prince Charles and Diana. Fortunately, it was in July and turned out to be a beautiful day, we had spent weeks making bunting and decorations with the residents and there was a buzz of excitement. The wedding was in the morning and we all crowded into the big lounge to watch it together amid lots of 'Ooohs' and 'Aaaahs', especially when Diana emerged in her spectacular princess type wedding dress!

We had lunch in the garden and were later joined by friends and family members for fun, games, music, singing, dancing and merrymaking and a great time was had by all.

Chapter 5

The beauty of Sunnymount, and something I really related to, was the fact that they encouraged contact with animals. We were allowed to take our pets to work, they had sheep and goats and there were the chickens which provided eggs for the home and to sell.

Gerald had a phone call one day from a girl who had heard of us through Friends of Sunnymount, she had a pony she wanted to donate to the Home. I was the only member of staff who had had much contact with horses, so I was called to the office and asked to investigate the offer. Debbie's father had racehorses, but Debbie didn't take after her father rather resenting the time and money spent on them. Life is odd, my parents would have loved to have a daughter like Debbie, and I would have given the moon to have been born into a horsy family! Maybe my passion for horses was born out of the fact I had to fight and work hard to have them in my life.

I spoke to the girl and arranged to meet her and go and see the pony. Helen was a young attractive girl, but she said she was studying and didn't have the time or money to dedicate to Peggy her pony.

Peggy was turned out on common land somewhere near Coventry. She was a pretty, little grey mare about 13:2hands high a typical native pony but with quite nice confirmation and good bone. The English native breeds are usually tough and strong even though they are not very big they can carry a farmer all day over the hills and moors checking the livestock. Helen caught Peggy with no problem, her legs were clean, and she was good to handle, she trotted up sound, just her feet and teeth needed some attention and she probably needed worming and vaccinating. Helen tacked her up out there in the open with other loose horses; they stood about looking on curiously at our antics with their friend. We both had a little ride and she was comfortable and although not highly schooled she was fairly obedient. Helen said she would include the tack, a snaffle bridle and all-purpose saddle.

I reported back to the boss who was going to consult the committee. They reported back with enthusiasm the condition being I took full responsibility for the care of the pony and supervision of riding, for which fortunately I was qualified. I was delighted at the prospect although I knew I would have to be careful to organise it in my own time, only involving residents when I was on duty when appropriate and if approved by the senior member of staff on duty.

Helen true to her word organised transport and duly arrived with Peggy and her gear. There was great excitement, we had previously bought water and feed buckets and a supply of feed and some hay. There was a shelter at the bottom of the field to use as a feed store and I had made room in my garage for the tack.

All the staff and residents flocked outside and were anxious to meet the new arrival. I was cautious as I didn't know how the pony would react to such a reception committee, so made sure everyone stood well back while we unloaded her, and I led her into the field and closed the gate. I then allowed those who showed interest to come and pat her one at a time. Their reactions were mixed but almost all positive, Hilary for example was grinning from ear to ear and repeating Peggy's name with intermittent giggles and clinging to the fence, she didn't want to come too near but was fascinated and didn't want to leave her either when it was time to go back to the house.

Some were excited but with a very short span of concentration like Katy and John, they wanted to keep rushing up to pat her, it was important to encourage them to slow down in order not to startle her and they soon got the message and seemed anxious to learn, they busied themselves telling the others what to do and why. The Downs children, notable loving, were so gentle and it was obviously, love at first sight. We only had one pony and 30 residents so we would start with only those who showed the most interest.

Gerald would definitely be one of the initial groups and his reaction was probably the most surprising, he was generally a bit rough and grumpy, he was frustrated, with his cleft palate communication was difficult as we had difficulty understanding him and he was a young man who knew exactly what he wanted. He was so gentle with Peggy, with his head on one side he very gently stroked and stroked her neck, and he didn't want to leave her. The blind girls loved the feel of her coat and the musty smell of her breath, they couldn't see her, but their other senses seemed much finer than ours, they felt the velvet softness of her muzzle, the silky feel of her summer coat and her rather bristly mane.

Little Susanne was fascinated but nervous, she desperately wanted to come near but was obviously frightened, when she finally touched Peggy's shoulder with my hand on her hand she squealed with delight.

First Peggy needed some attention, and I had no horsey contacts in the area, so I went to a nearby farm where I had seen horses. The main farmyard was used as a racing yard and full of racehorses, at the side there was a smaller yard where there were some private horses owned by Jo who was a prominent dressage rider, I had read about her success in the local paper. It seemed a bit cheeky, but I went around, and explained that we had acquired a pony and asked if she could recommend a good horse vet and a blacksmith. She was so friendly and helpful, in due course Jack the vet came and checked Peggy over, filed her teeth, vaccinated and wormed her then Ken the blacksmith a gentle giant and such a kind man came and shod Peggy for us.

The shoeing was an unusual experience for the small group watching, it was evident that they had mixed feelings about what this great big man was going to do to their beloved pony. To see Ken heating the shoe until it was red hot, placing it on Peggy's hoof amid sizzling and smoke and then beating it into the correct shape on his anvil, then fitting it again with the strange smell of singing hoof and the smoke, which made more than one of the onlookers wrinkle their noses. When he dropped the shoe into a bucket of cold water it sizzled and spluttered as the red, hot shoe hit the cold water to cool it off before nailing it to her hoof and filing the whole thing smooth. Peggy was as good as gold and stood quietly on three legs like a veteran. I told them they would be learning how to pick her feet up and clean her hooves then oiling them, more than one of them looked at me in total disbelief. Afterwards I told them Ken was an exceptionally good blacksmith, which he was, and how Peggy would now be much more comfortable taking them for rides down the road. On hearing this little Gerald who had been looking concerned and a little agitated throughout the whole process rushed up to Ken and hugged him around the legs with such enthusiasm that we couldn't persuade him to let Ken go. We had difficulty extricating him luckily Ken was rather touched and mildly amused.

It was clear that I could not begin teaching them to ride without assistance, initially several members of staff offered to help and they too had to be initiated regarding safety when being around horses. We wanted our prospective riders to gain confidence, so we began with grooming, leading in hand and of course cleaning tack and oiling hooves. Geoffrey treated Peggy as he did the shoes and would have brushed her all day long, fortunately she did not seem to mind. Gerald was very quick to learn how to pick up her feet and clean them, being a bit gruff he was firm but gentle and he and Peggy understood each other from the moment they met, I should think she had never been groomed so much in all her life as during her first week at Sunnymount.

I had to make a safe mounting block to facilitate mounting and dismounting, initially John, Katy, Gerald and Geoffrey were the first to brave the new adventure.

Michael, Johnny and Suzanna watched in awe, but were not yet brave enough to try.

Riding gave our charges a whole new perspective in life, for the first time they were looking down at us and this gave them a sense of freedom. For those with less mobility to be able to go around the field, touch the leaves on the trees and move effortlessly was liberating.

We began very slowly just getting them on and off and confident to sit on the pony without clinging to the saddle, to stroke and pat her and relax before we moved off. I had a helper on each side to start with a hand on the rider's knee and strict instructions to keep level with the pony's shoulder if possible. As the riders gained confidence the helpers took their hands away but continued walking alongside. Little by little the riders felt confident without holding onto the saddle and learned to hold the reins and begin to control Peggy. For some a short walk was more than enough and for others they wanted to trot and canter straight away. For some it was a question of building confidence and others controlling their impulse to canter off across the field before they were safe in trot.

We learned that if little Gerald was missing at mealtimes, bearing in mind he loved his food, he was sure to be found in the field talking to Peggy. Hilary never wanted to ride but she loved to help me with feeding watering and grooming. Michael, Johnny and Susanne all plucked up enough courage to ride and although nervous were obviously thrilled with their achievement. It was perfect to take them one at a time as they were all at different levels and had different needs. Staggering the riders also meant the workload for Peggy was not too great and she could give pleasure to so many.

Word spread and another girl approached us, she had an old pony who was still sound, and she was looking for a good home for him. She lived locally and had the pony in a field nearby, so I went to see him, he was a bit bigger than Peggy, not handsome but quite stocky like a cob, he had plenty of bone which meant he could carry a bigger and heavier rider. He was quiet and friendly if a little lazy but that meant that he would be safe for the riders to begin to ride unaided as Peggy was a little fast for some, so I had to be careful when letting her off the leading rein.

It would also be nice for Peggy to have company as horses are herd animals and really should not be kept alone in fact, I have heard that in some countries it is illegal, although this is not so in England and to be honest Peggy had settled in well without another equine for company. In fact, she was hardly ever alone, she had the sheep for company and Peter and Tommy were up and down her field tending to the chickens who also clucked around her when she was grazing. I tended to her twice a day, not to mention the riding sessions which happened most days. Besides there was nearly always someone leaning over the gate just gazing at her or chattering to her, so she did not have time to be lonely.

We had approval from the committee and Joey arrived. He was quite poor when he came; partly the time of year he was changing his coat after the winter and he had a big frame so he looked rather bony, but I loved feeding horses up and was convinced that in a short time he would look like a different animal, which he did. He soon became fat and shiny and was a huge success as Mick and Tommy and other larger or heavier residents could ride too.

Gerald our Administrator showed enthusiasm and expressed a desire to ride one of the ponies. He was obviously a novice rider and chose to ride Peggy leaving me to ride Joey. He probably chose her because she was the smallest but in fact Joey would have been easier for him to manage, however, he could not be dissuaded from riding Peggy. It is a known fact that horses react to the state of mind of their rider, Peggy who was good as gold with the residents even if they were nervous but proved to be quite stubborn with the boss when he tried to tell her what to do, after many failed attempts he managed to convince Peggy to follow Joey and me over a small jump, all this to the hysterical laughter mixed with applause from the residents and staff alike, luckily he took it all in good spirits.

As we all gained confidence it was great to have two people riding together and we started having little bending races, walking races, obstacle courses and generally fun on horseback. Tracey and Angela the little blind girls also started riding and the freedom of movement without having to worry about bumping into things was liberating and I couldn´t help but admire them as they were so brave and trusting.

The ponies looked well and had become firm friends, it was good to see them, grazing together or standing in the shade scratching each other's withers, this brought hoots of laughter from the residents, even more so when I showed them how to scratch the pony´s withers which caused them stretched out their necks and pout their top lips in ecstasy.

I had an anxious moment when I saw the lads building a huge bonfire in the field and my fears were confirmed. Yes, I was told; there were plans for a big party on bonfire night with fireworks and barbeque to take place in the field'. I can only think that they thought the ponies would enjoy the party, but I panicked at the thought, bonfire night is a nightmare for animals and wildlife.

I rushed down the lane to see Jo who had helped me before with advice regarding the vet and blacksmith. I explained the situation and asked if there was anywhere that I could put the ponies for the night. As always, she came up trumps, there was a mare and foal in a little paddock and Jo said they came in at night so the ponies could go there so long as I could collect them in the morning. What a relief!

Peggy and Joey were doing a good job, it wasn't only the riding, but the caring, grooming, feeding, watering and even cleaning the tack, each resident had learned some new skill and had enjoyed some aspect regarding the ponies even if they didn't want to ride.

Chapter 6

The word spread regarding the ponies and riding at Sunnymount and I was receiving requests from the Special School, the Training Centre also parents who brought their children to Sunnymount for short stay who were keen for their children to ride. It was clear it was becoming far too much work for Peggy and Joey.

Prior to working at Sunnymount I had been a helper and later Instructor for an R.D.A group. The Riding for the Disabled Association was started after the Second World War when people began to realise the therapeutic benefit of riding, for people with both physical and mental problems. The Winford Orthopaedic Hospital found riding helped their patients who were both physically and mentally traumatised; it noticeably speeded their physical recovery and affected their state of mind restoring their confidence in the future.

In 1952, Lis Hartel, a Danish dressage rider, won the silver medal in the Olympics for dressage although she had no use in her lower legs, anyone who has ridden dressage understands what an amazing feat this was. This really spurred on the whole concept of the therapy and as a result pony riding for disabled children began at Chigwell. Later the Polio Fellowship instigated riding for polio sufferers and eventually an Advisory Council for Riding for the Disabled was formed following which groups began to spring up all over the country. In 1969, this Council was revised and the Riding for the Disabled Association, R.D.A as we know it today was formed with H.R.H Princess Anne as their Patron and she later became President in 1976, she still holds the position today. They not only provide horse riding but also horse vaulting, carriage driving and other equine assisted therapies. Horses have also visited very sick people in hospital or at home and appear to have a special empathy for people suffering from all kinds of problems. It is also true that animals in general seem to be therapeutic and beneficial to humans in need of comfort and healing.

I contacted the R.D.A enquiring about groups in our area, there was a group but quite a distance away and unable to take on more riders, so the logical conclusion was to form our own group. What I needed was to find was a local riding school willing to take us on. Eventually I found a small Riding School in the same area as the Special School and the Training Centre. Barn Cottage was run by Jean and Peter Coleman it was quite small but had a safe outdoor arena and half a dozen quiet horses and ponies we could use.

We negotiated reasonable terms and I realised we would have to start fund raising as well as organising the groups. Initially I booked two groups a week, one for children from Hazeloak Special School and one for those from Oakenshaw Training Centre. Those who had approached me individually I took on at Sunnymount. This was becoming a second, full time job!

We officially became The Solihull Group for Riding for the Disabled. The next item on the agenda was to find volunteers and train them, Friends of Sunnymount gave me a hand here, plus word of mouth in the locality and as a result I made some good new friends.

I was on duty one morning as we were between cooks, so everyone was giving a helping hand. I was peeling onions at the kitchen sink with Edna, our oldest resident, when Daphne showed a new prospective R.D.A. helper through to the kitchen. Claire not only became a huge asset to the group but also a firm friend. She was a horse owner so had knowledge and experience with horses what is more she proved to be an excellent secretary and fund raiser. Claire was not put off by the rather unorthodox introduction in fact she joined in asking for a knife and helped us to peel the onions amid floods of tears and much laughter.

Claire was also indispensable for her talent in shepherding. When we wanted to take the ponies out of the field the sheep wanted to come with us and without Claire the operation was very tricky. Claire with great aplomb, as though she had been doing it all her life, grabbed the thick, curly wool around the sheep's neck with both hands, one on each side of her neck, then straddling her she guided her down the field amid much bleating at being separated from her friends, meanwhile while we opened the gate and took the ponies out safely. From behind they looked most comical it looked as though Claire was riding the sheep, luckily, she had extremely long legs!

Jayne Parsloe, whose daughter had a horse and competed, meaning she was also used to handling horses also volunteered, she was reliable and regular also living locally, so she became tower of strength. Elizabeth Wigglesworth was another delightful lady who related well to the riders; she was full of empathy and understanding. Jean Singleton also became a stoic helper and supporter, we were so fortunate to have these lovely people join our team of volunteers. Joy Noad lived nearby, she was retired but had had a small riding school and to my surprise she had been one of my teachers at Junior School. I had been terribly shy when I was young and I remember I had been terrified of her. I rode at another riding school belonging to a work colleague of my mother's. I had a series of quite nasty falls between the ages of seven and ten, in one such fall I fell off the pony and bit the tarmac. When I appeared at school with broken front teeth and a split upper lip Miss Noad was understandably horrified, her disapproval was such that I felt guilty as well as injured. Yet she proved to be a good lady, perhaps her manner was brusque, but her heart was in the right place. She still had a stable and a pony and helped us in many ways proving to be both generous and efficient also kind in her own way.

Peter from Barn Cottage was able to teach the groups when I was working and so I concentrated on the regular riding of the Sunnymount residents we planned weekly around my shifts and according to the availability of helpers. Barn Cottage also helped us with a Gala for the royal wedding where all the ponies were plaited and looked very smart. Ted Edgar a local and famous, international showjumper was invited. He kindly accepted and presented all the riders with a rosette, he was good fun and a little bit cheeky with Jean, he definitely added a sparkle to the day.

We took a group of riders to the Horseman's Service held at Solihull Riding Club and this was an opportunity for them to see and meet more horses and mix with able bodied riders. Little Gerald wanted to take one horse and rider home with him, fortunately the rider was both amused and flattered.

An R.D.A riding holiday was held at Preston Baggot at the beautiful home of a delightful lady called Mary Jones. I had been there years previously to teach at a Pony Club Camp, but this was to be a very, special camp and great opportunity for our disabled riders. They were to stay over a period of several days, living together and looking after the ponies with lots of activities and competitions. Healthy, happy days!

There were the regular riders, the occasional short stay who wanted to ride, or individuals who applied referred to us from the R.D.A. One such rider was Jan, an amazing girl who suffered from spasticity which was caused by damage to the brain or spinal cord, although it sometimes occurs as a result of Cerebral Palsy or Multiple Sclerosis amongst other causes. Spasticity is caused by an imbalance of the signals from the central nervous system to the muscles.

Jan's speech and mobility were quite severely impaired, although she made herself understood over the phone, not without difficulty and because she was a determined young lady. I took as many details as possible and we made an appointment for her to come and meet us and discuss the possibilities, meanwhile I contacted Christine Jones, our physiotherapist, for her opinion and advice. She told me a horse-riding simulator had proved beneficial for children with Cerebral palsy with noticeable improvement of their static and dynamic balance. Their sitting ability showed a particularly significant improvement. In Taiwan of all places a clinical trial had taken place with 30 children with cerebral palsy, half using the simulator and half riding ponies, the horseback riding group had showed the most improvement so the simulator was considered to be a good surrogate for riding real horses when horseback riding was not available.

Stretching exercises also help with posture control and motor function and these are much more pleasant in the open air on a pony, not to mention the psychological effects and motivation. Another important factor having a strong psychological impact is the freedom of movement the pony gives to people who struggle with mobility, the ability to move freely and effortlessly through countryside which was previously inaccessible for them in a wheelchair gives them a completely new viewpoint, being able to see everything literally and metaphorically from a different perspective. I was really beginning to understand the far-reaching benefits of riding for people struggling with disabilities. Nature is salubrious for everyone but even more so for those suffering from disabilities.

Children who had had Riding therapy in addition to their rehab showed a marked improvement in a matter of a few weeks, the passive hip abduction induced by sitting astride a pony significantly improved hip adduction spasticity, sitting astride a pony or horse held the thighs in passive abduction and this in turn improved mobility and reduced pain, so we were really, excited to see if riding would help Jan.

When I first met Jan, I was a little taken aback as she was rather tall, and I wondered how she would manage with the ponies. When you ride a horse or pony that is too small for you, there is a tendency for your lower leg to swing as there is no contact with the horse's side and this in turn can affect your balance, but as it happened, she was fine, and she was so thin she in fact weighed less than some of our Down children. I also wondered how the ponies would react to her involuntary jerky movements, however I need not have worried we decided to try Peggy at first as she was nearer to the ground so easier for us to help Jan.

Thanks to Claire some local undertakers had made us a very splendid mobile mounting block which was a vast improvement on my makeshift one. it had handles so was portable and had steps that slid inside making it compact to transport, not only a work of art but an indispensable piece of equipment especially as were beginning to attend events and it was much better quality than the one, we had originally put together. Peggy stood like a rock while we helped Jan onto the mounting block, she had never ridden before but obviously had a natural affinity with animals from the way she talked to Peggy apart from which she was fearless. Initially I attached the reins to the head-collar and the bit so assuring Jan that she would not hurt Peggy if her movements were too brusque. Jan was intelligent and quick to learn, she made terrific progress her balance improved with each session and she seemed to have better balance on the pony than off.

We were surprised one day when she didn't turn up for her ride and we hadn't received a message. Later it transpired she had been ill and was detained at the hospital, so Carlos and I decided to pay her a visit and take her some shopping. Jan lived alone in a small ground floor flat where she invited us in and insisted, we had tea and biscuits. It was very humbling to see how she was so determined to live as normal a life as possible, she had a few gadgets to help her like a kettle that tipped so she didn't have to lift and pour the boiling water, which would have been virtually impossible as well as dangerous. She drank through a straw, to lift a cup to her mouth it would have been almost impossible for her to do so without spilling half of the contents, to be honest I had never really considered how difficult the simplest and most mundane tasks must be for her. We had an interesting afternoon with her. She had a supportive family, but she was determined not to be a burden so she had applied to the local council and secured the flat at a low rent. Furthermore, she worked, she had managed to get a job in a factory so she made her packed lunch every morning and went to work on the bus. Bearing in mind the slightest task required a huge effort she was incredibly independent and our admiration for her grew by the minute. Sadly, people can be very cruel and inevitably in the factory environment she had suffered some ridicule and unkindness, however, Jan had a positive attitude and was not riled by such situations she merely put it down to ignorance and remained totally unruffled. When I thought how I got indignant and defensive over the slightest criticism I felt quite ashamed and very humbled before this brave girl. She not only rode regularly but loved to get involved with our fund-raising activities, which gave her some social life and fun among people who not only understood and admired her but became her friends.

We later discovered that Jan also helped local disabled people despite being disabled herself in fact she did an amazing amount of voluntary work in the borough. Three local Lions groups were so impressed they clubbed together and bought her a tricycle to help her move around her community more easily. They presented it to Jan at Christmas to her surprise and delight and it was followed by a photograph in the local newspaper together with a detailed report of all her good work, we were all surprised and impressed as she had never spoken much of all her activities in the community.

Peggy and Joey worked all day giving pony rides at the Annual Garden Fete to raise funds, Claire also bought her horse Topper over to give a hand, Topper was a bit of a lad, he had a huge buck and poor Claire had hit the deck on more than one occasion, but butter wouldn't melt in his mouth when giving the children rides.

We all attended a Mid-Summer's Evening in Knowle to raise funds, we had some pub suppers with raffles and quizzes, and we had collecting boxes in shops and pubs in the area, which little by little accumulated a substantial amount of money from people's small change and generosity.

I had a rather ambitious idea for a period supper and evening at Packwood House, a local Tudor House, belonging to the National Trust, with a minstrel's gallery and a great hall all in a beautiful setting, and to my surprise we gained permission to use the house, I also knew a group of singers who sang madrigals which would be perfect for the setting. Unfortunately, my organisation skills were sadly lacking if not disastrous at the time. Ideas and enthusiasm I had in abundance but that was not sufficient to organise an event of this kind, it requires careful planning. A friend set up a P.A system, I had tickets printed and organised caterers, I thought I was doing well! Word spread and there was great enthusiasm, my first mistake was to print more tickets and sell tickets to more people than could comfortably be accommodated, a further consequence was that we ran short of food, Gerald had persuaded the mayor to attend and because they didn't go up to the buffet but waited at their table they nearly ended up with no food! I sent the singers up to the gallery and I was so busy trying to keep everyone happy I gave no introduction or thanks, the Mayor felt neglected, Gerald embarrassed and the poor singers were like background music, which was not only disgraceful but a pity as they were exceptionally good, there was so much merriment and everyone was making such a noise I should have called everyone to order, but I was tied up with the caterers, welcoming people as they arrived and seating them in groups. Some people had a great time eating and drinking more than their fair share whilst others hardly got a look in, we made a huge profit, but I had clearly lost control of proceedings and rather bungled what should have been a magical evening for all.

I sometimes got into trouble at work as I loved organising outings and activities but on occasions to the detriment of the day to day running of the home. While having my knuckles rapped, not for the first time, I was told it was clear I had never had a family or run a home! I would have to learn to plan better and keep the balance between efficient housekeeping and organising activities and outings.

I must say we had some lovely times and I never ceased to marvel at the reactions of our charges. I took them to a Donkey Sanctuary and the interaction was even easier with the donkeys than with the ponies as they were smaller and generally slower moving, also they drove some of the donkeys in tiny carts. We talked about the possibilities this could imply for people with limited mobility and later little carts were designed to hold a wheelchair, imagine the freedom that gave to someone confined to a wheelchair, to drive a donkey cart through the countryside. Later after I left Claire successfully set up a group for donkey driving in Balsall Common. The Duke of Edinburgh used to play Polo on horseback when he was young, but he gave it up and started driving horses when he was 50. It was not a tame sport, when he was competing, he had some horrendous accidents, but he was still driving into his eighties and even at ninety if a little more sedately. The queen too is still riding in her nineties, so it is a sport you can do at any level and still enjoy.

The headquarters for the R.D.A at that time was at Stoneleigh which was also host to the Royal Horse Show and they decided to hold competitions for disabled riders, there was a Mini Olympics Dressage Event. This was long before the Paralympics for Equestrian events. Pippa, a Downs girl who sometimes came to Sunnymount for short stay was riding regularly with us at Barn Cottage and was a promising rider. She had mastered the rising trot almost immediately; she was a neat little rider, managed the pony off the leading rein with no problem and had also started to canter. We had our own little competitions within the group, gymkhana was the most popular as everyone could take part, with or without helpers, there was much excitement, and everyone had fun. The riders who could now manage without leaders and helpers were beginning to manage small jumps, obstacle courses and we had started to practice simple dressage tests for which we had made our own letters for the arena.

We decided to enter Pippa in the competition at Stoneleigh. All the riders practiced plaiting the ponies' manes and tails and plaiting each other's hair or pieces of string and those who were able learned the test practicing on their feet or drawing pictures, it was a team project. We entered her in a class with a test in walk and trot, her mother had already bought her jodhpurs, long boots and a hat and I lent her my white stock and black jacket, the jacket was a bit big but looked fine when she was sitting on the pony.

Jean and Peter provided transport in the form of a Land Rover and trailer, we chose one of their ponies which Pippa had been riding regularly, and off we went, followed by a minibus full of supporters. Pippa was nervous but the rules were flexible, for example they could have a leader and helper or verbal assistance, being marked accordingly. Pippa was early in the competition, she was about the third to compete, the previous two riders had their trainers in the arena with them, so I did likewise with Pippa, and she rode a nice, neat test. Later in the competition some of the riders completed the test completely unaided, which gained them extra points, and if I hadn't been so overanxious Pippa could have managed perfectly well on her own. She was not placed but they all received a rosette, Pippa was happy she was beaming from ear to ear and could not stop hugging and kissing her pony and bowing to her fan club, so another great day was had by all.

The RDA later organised a Gymkhana at Stoneleigh, this time Jo took the ponies for us in her super big horsebox which caused considerable excitement. Jan competed on Peggy who had her mane painstakingly plaited and really looked quite splendid. All the ponies were well turned out. The ponies had a different rider for each event so everyone had an opportunity and all the competitors received rosettes, so another great day was had by all.

There was also a local Horse Show at Woodlands with lots of special classes for leading rein, mostly gymkhana events which our riders had been practicing and loved. Another exhausting but extremely satisfying day, one of our riders was so determined and she won three rosettes, not firsts but it didn't matter to her, she couldn't stop grinning, for her it was the achievement of a lifetime.

Sometimes we took Peggy and Joey down the lane to the ford where we had a picnic. We were joined by the others who drove down to join us bringing the food and spreading out the picnic on the soft grass.

It was a pleasant way to spend a summer afternoon enjoyed by the ponies too who tucked into the lush grass alongside the stream, the children would take it in turns to hold their lead ropes which was quite safe as the ponies were going nowhere with such a delicious feast at their feet. Then they would take it in turns to ride home, some walking, some riding and some preferring the minibus.

The group continued well after I left, thanks to Claire and my father (who took over as chairman). However, Claire was secretary, organiser, and fund-raiser; she worked wonders and even kept in touch with some of the children years later and discovered how riding had enriched their lives. The group also had their photograph in the paper with Red Rum, the famous racehorse who won the Grand National three, times. In his retirement he spent his time travelling up and down the country appearing at functions to raise money for charity. He still drew the crowds; he knew he was special and posed with his groom for photographs with the children.

Moya was a little girl with little or no communication skills and poor concentration. The experts had said they could do no more to help her but her determined mother contacted us to see whether we would consider letting her try riding. Of course, we said we were happy to try, on studying her case we were told pony rides only; with maximum caution.

Contact with the pony and nature helped her state of mind, she seemed happy with Peggy. Claire showed endless patience and although verbal instructions were of little use Claire talked all the time, showing her what to do by tapping her hand and demonstrating, by doing this Moya learned to pat her pony and later hold the reins. Claire kept in touch with Moya's mother and when we had all moved on many years later, she told me Moya was still enjoying her riding.

Chapter 7

Irish Claire, our deputy matron, was expecting a baby so was due to leave under happy circumstances and she left with a baby shower together with much well wishing. Claire had been excellent at her job I had liked her approach and learned a lot from her so was saddened to see her go. However, it did mean promotion was in the air, so I became a senior housemother having charge of a family group and small team of staff. This I took very seriously and began to take far more interest in the domestic aspects and responsibilities, diet, general health, exercise and trying to develop any talents or interests of our family members. This also meant I could communicate directly with the doctors, teachers, psychologists and physiotherapists to try to better understand my charges and offer support and back-up.

Our physiotherapist, Christine Jones was organising a Reflexology course and was keen for someone working with people with disabilities to take part. Christine was convinced this kind of natural therapy could prove beneficial for people with all kinds of disabilities especially if we could begin when they were children, the younger the better.

Some medical knowledge was required, in order to participate and as I had completed the chiropody course I was accepted. The chiropody course had included quite in-depth anatomy and physiology, we had to study bone structure, muscle, nerve and skin functions and malfunctions. There would be far better qualified people on the course, but it would be a challenge and I had always had a leaning towards Natural Medicine and Therapies although I knew precious little about them.

The course was held at Christine's home, a delightful and spacious farm-house she also had a smallholding and a few sheep. There were about a dozen of us on the course from all walks of life, a few doctors, nurses, midwives, a homeopath and even a hypnotherapist. It was all very, interesting, but I was a little tongue in cheek wondering if I would be out of my depth, bearing in mind that I had never been a particularly good student. The course was held over a series of long weekends, three long intensive days of lectures with plenty of homework in between. I had mentioned it at work, and they were both helpful and enthusiastic encouraging me to go ahead, they re-organised my shifts so by taking just a few days holiday I was able to attend the whole course.

Reflexology is treating the whole body and its problems through massaging the feet. This is not as cuckoo as it sounds; we walk on our feet and are held on this earth by gravity. In fact, there are nerve endings in the soles of the feet connected to all parts of the body. The principle is rather like acupuncture, which works on the nervous system using needles to stimulate sensory nerves under the skin at points all over the body, so stimulating the body to produce natural substances, such as pain-relieving endorphins and promoting the natural self-healing process.

Reflexology only uses massage or pressure mainly on parts of the feet but also on the hands and head. As I understood it this was also working through the nervous system which in turn connected to all parts of the body, having studied feet I realised how complex they are. In the foot there are 26 bones, a quarter of the number of bones in the whole body, 33 joints and hundreds of muscles, tendons and ligaments not to mention the nerves. There are 7,000 nerve endings in the feet which carry the messages to and from all parts of the body and the brain, so helping everything to work in harmony. Not to mention 250,000 sweat glands so it is not surprising that many of us suffer from sweaty feet! The human body is incredibly complex and fascinating.

Christine explained that the nervous system is rather like an electric circuit when there is a block or malfunction it creates havoc. We have all experienced for example when you break or have a problem with one leg it puts tremendous strain on the other leg, in turn putting us out of balance which may cause hip and back problems. It seemed logical that the same applies to our internal organs and systems.

We are even more complex because we are all so different, identical physical conditions are felt and coped with entirely differently by each person. Here state of mind comes into play, and Jan and many of our disabled friends are shining examples of this so often those of us with the least problems complain the most!

We had to study all the systems of the body, as they are all reflected in the feet. Then we had to study the most common ailments and dysfunctions and learn the order of treatment. The theory being that the massage or pressure relaxes the nerves and unblocks the system allowing the body to right itself and so function correctly, at least this was my understanding. A typical example being when a person has kidney stones if you relax the kidney first and the stone begins to move but if the ureter is still tight you can cause even greater pain, so one always works from the outside in, the same with the digestive system and the heart is always the last to be treated.

I had learned foot massage with the chiropody course, but this was a totally different approach, the only thing they had in common was the effleurage, long strokes of massage to send the loosened rubbish towards the lymph glands to be dealt with and eliminated accordingly.

I enjoyed the course, apart from the material which was fascinating we were in lovely surroundings with interesting people and fabulous vegetarian food at lunchtime, all included, it was like a mini holiday.

When it came to the practical aspect, I had a slight problem as I was extremely ticklish and hated having my feet touched. This required paramount self-control on my part in order not to kick my colleague in the teeth. I had always suffered from this problem and foot inspection at school had been a nightmare! However, I survived, I was fortunate enough to have been assigned a very understanding and patient partner.

It really sounds strange, but with practice you get a real feel for the person´s whole body and organs through the feet. At the very least it is pleasant and relaxing, and most people enjoy the treatment, the effects are not immediate, but it does seem to have extremely positive results for some people. People also relax and talk while being treated and this alone is an additional therapy, when people relax, they often open-up, and feel they can spill out all their fears and problems to a complete stranger, who neither knows them personally nor will judge them, and there is no truer saying than: ´A problem shared is a problem halved.´

So, with my brand-new certificate I launched into practice. Already several of my chiropody clients had shown an interest, and I also had permission to practice on some of our residents at Sunnymount. The latter proved very receptive, in fact once they had received a treatment they wanted more and more, I suppose in part it was due to the personal one to one attention, whatever the reason it was very gratifying to work with them. I also noticed that for some more highly strung people Reflexology had a very calming effect and was certainly preferable to giving them so much medication.

The local doctor was young and open minded, he also recommended me to some of his patients. They were mostly elderly people who suffered from chronic conditions like arthritis or depression, I like to think they benefitted considerably, although obviously a complete cure was out of the question. However, if it improved their quality of life and they enjoyed the experience it was certainly worthwhile.

Johnny, in particular, loved having his feet done, he was so sweet and could wrap me around his little finger, when I was on night duty he would come and wrap his arms around my waist saying, "Judy, I can't sleep…please, can you do my feet?"

How could I resist! His friend, Annie, who was terrified of having her toenails cut would watch nervously, eventually she asked me to massage her feet, she still held tightly to her own foot, but it was progress indeed.

Soon more promotion was in the offing, this time to the position of Assistant Matron. This involved more training and Maggie, and I were sent on a Management course, it was some way away and I drove, we never went the same way twice, I never really understood how we got there but fortunately we allowed plenty of time so were never late. The course was interesting, we covered motivation, organisation, teamwork, managing difficult situations etc. There were a lot of group workshops and psychology involved. Maggie and I enjoyed it, whether we would be capable of putting it into practice would be another matter.

Another of my new tasks was to do the wages, I was happy with this arrangement as I had always liked working with figures. There were about 30 members of staff and each one had to be worked out separately, initially the system seemed so complex, I wondered why it could not be simplified. I ended up taking it home to do quietly in the evening because with so much going on at work I was afraid of making a mistake. Even if I chose a quiet time and closed the office door it was impossible to avoid interruptions.

Another new responsibility was the medication. The medicine cabinet was kept locked in the office. After meals, the residents formed a queue outside the office to receive their medicine. Sadly, most of them were on some sort of medication, but there were regular checks and meetings to review their dosage and the aim was to keep it to a minimum. There was one little girl on insulin, so we had to test her level, control he diet and inject her, but she never complained, she accepted her situation and the injections with no fuss as a normal part of life.

When the time came, we also had to administer their flu jabs. I had injected horses for years but that was a slightly different technique, a horse's skin is thicker than that of a human. We would give the horse a hearty pat on the muscle to be injected and wop in the needle applying the syringe once the needle had been inserted and the horse had relaxed. Before giving intra-muscular injections to people we had to practice on an orange, and then on each other it was a slower gentler process than injecting horses!

Hilary was terrified of needles and went into a panic when she realised everyone was having their flu jab. Gerald's technique rather shocked us but maybe it was the only way. He told her not to worry it wasn't for her and then went up behind her and popped in the dose through her clothes rather the way we injected horses, it was a tiny quantity and a thin liquid, so it was over in a flash. I couldn't help questioning how hygienic or effective this was but fortunately she suffered no adverse reaction.

Little by little money had been raised and we were able to open a new unit. It was to be a small unit for a group of four profoundly disabled children. They were all wheelchair bound, so needed ramps, hoists and pulleys with a special bathroom and wet room. This would be staffed separately, as qualified nursing staff was required. This unit was created in what had been the games room and outbuildings beneath our flat.

Maggie and I went on work experience to gain practical experience regarding handling, rehabilitation, physiotherapy etc. for such children. Some cases were heart-breaking and the pain, both psychological and physical, these profoundly disabled children must suffer is unimaginable. One small child wore mittens as he scratched his nose to such a degree, he no longer had a nose, just two holes in a very sore looking area on his face. I accompanied one child to have water therapy, there were shallow pools where they could lie and splash in warm water and this brought a little light to his eyes which were otherwise withdrawn and sad.

Our more able-bodied charges showed both interest and compassion for their new neighbours. Many of us feel uncomfortable in the company of the profoundly disabled, probably because for years they have been kept isolated from society shut away in special institutions. Prior to that some lived in the community, there was always the village idiot, who was probably some poor brain damaged soul. The more profoundly handicapped were shut away from society in Institutions, thank goodness things have changed.

We have the wonderful example of Stephen Hawkins, who despite tremendous physical disabilities focused on his research and teaching. He also transmitted the message that he wanted to be treated the same as everyone else, with neither compassion nor embarrassment. When he realised there was no hope and his expectations had been reduced to zero, he treated every day as a bonus and appreciated the smallest things. He achieved more in his lifetime than most of us could ever dream of. We should all take a leaf out of his book.

One little boy in the new unit wanted to ride, well his parents wanted him to ride as Tony was usually confined to a wheelchair. I had seen basket saddles years gone used by tiny children who were propped up in the basket saddles and put on a pony at a very tender age. I had seen a similar saddle used by the RDA. However, Tony to our surprise managed without such drastic equipment as it was mainly his legs which did not function; he just had to wear his own helmet which he wore most of the time anyway. Imagine the freedom of moving on a pony, looking down on everyone else, after being confined to a wheelchair when everyone looks down at you, it was obviously uplifting from the expression on the little boy's face and the excitement he showed when he saw the pony.

Another very disabled little boy also began riding at the request of his parents, he wore a special belt with handles and a helper each side to steady him. We had to lift him onto the pony, he showed no resistance and strangely we felt he was benefitting in his own way at his own level and although he had no communication with us, he did relate to the pony and she to him.

Another course came up through Christine the physiotherapist, it was loosely related to the reflexology using the same principal of massage on Feet hands and head, but only treating the bone structures concentrating on the spine. The spine encases the Spinal Cord, which is our central nervous system. This goes right up to our brain and has spinal nerves branching out and leading to all parts of the body. The technique was titled Metamorphosis (meaning change) or Pre-Natal Therapy, again Christine was anxious for disabled people to have the opportunity to try new therapies.

The course was given by a tall, handsome French man. Whilst working with Reflexology Robert St John discovered the relationship between the prenatal development and the spinal reflexes on the feet.

From working with disabled people, I knew only too well that problems occurring during pregnancy or a traumatic birth were often extremely damaging having a negative effect on the person's whole life. It seemed logical that to a lesser degree we are all born with blocks and defects of which we may be unaware but can affect our lives. If a pregnant mother has an illness, trauma or accident it is bound to have some effect on the development of the baby, also depending on the stage of growth of the foetus at the time of the trauma. This theory seemed feasible enough.

Going even deeper he told us that our physical, mental, emotional and behavioural problems are a reflection of underlying stress and can be accessed and alleviated through the reflex points. He stressed the importance of working with pregnant women and the benefits for mother and child.

It is beneficial for anyone of any age or condition, it is just that working with pregnant women gives a child a better start to lead a fuller, happier and healthier life, also working with the children themselves, the younger the better.

Another of his theories, which I agreed with one hundred percent, was the tendency of modern medicine to treat the symptoms and not the underlying problem.

Today we tend to use antibiotics, painkillers, anti-inflammatories, or cortisone for a multitude of ailments, when in simple terms we know for example: constipation or gastric disturbance can cause a headache, but painkillers for the headache don't cure constipation! This doesn't mean modern medicine has no role; in fact, it is amazing what can be done these days, and if you have a compound fracture, need a new heart valve or an organ transplant there are wonderful life-saving options available today.

I saw this more as a way of enhancing quality of life, and by unblocking lifelong stress in the body. Robert told us of considerable changes that had taken place when Metamorphosis was practiced on Autistic and Down's syndrome children within their first five years. It works with stress patterns which in turn can change the pattern of our lives.

Another attractive aspect of this treatment is its simplicity, it is safe easy to learn and does not require medical knowledge as you are not working on any organs, systems or ailments, simply relieving stress.

Robert told us a delightful story about a Down syndrome boy and a profoundly handicapped man in a vegetative state. They were partaking in a clinical trial in a Mental Institution. A boy with Down syndrome was fascinated and followed Robert as he gave treatment to a series of inmates. Like most children with Down syndrome he was friendly, open and affectionate so Robert taught him how to massage the feet of the poor soul who was bed ridden and in a vegetative state with no apparent communication with or reaction to anyone or anything. He supervised the boy for a few days and then gave him specific instructions as to when and for how long to treat the man. The boy was both consistent and meticulous, staff monitored from a distance and observed.

After some weeks, the man being treated was focusing on the door and his eyes followed the boy all the time he was in the room, this was a total breakthrough for someone who had never shown any response to anything or anybody in his whole life. Later he began to make noises when he saw the boy. Robert pointed out that if only that man had been treated from birth, how different his life might have been.

The human being is an amazing species as we have all the tools within our bodies to deal with all manner of adversities. Just think how a baby forms, skin heals a cut, the blood cells fight infection, broken bones knit, we need more medical help today because we have brought a lot of problems upon ourselves, stress, poor diet, and pollution being but a few common factors. Not only the human but all of nature's billions of species are truly incredible and the concept of removing blocks and allowing nature to take its course I found more appealing than trying to interfere with symptoms. The mere one to one situation of giving massage helps people to relax and feel that someone cares which affects their state of mind and in turn their physical condition.

This was no miracle cure but its simplicity and availability to all was a concept I warmed to. Robert said we should encourage people to treat each other, however, in practice people loved receiving treatment but were reluctant to practice it themselves probably many people have an aversion to feet, just like my own mother! Once more my so-called disabled friends were far more open to trying this new experience than the supposedly normal and able-bodied folk.

As I mentioned previously people with physical and mental disabilities had taught me so much and certainly proved that it is not what happens to us in life that is important but how we deal with it. Seeing the glass half full or half empty, focusing on the positive or the negative has a huge bearing on how our lives evolve. We are so busy mulling over the past or planning and worrying about the future we miss the magic of the present.

Some factors are undoubtedly in our genes as my father always affirmed, our family surroundings, upbringing and education undoubtedly influence us, but also our state of mind is fundamental for the direction of our lives.

I just want to express my heartfelt gratitude to these amazing people who changed my state of mind for the better, gave me gave me greater insight, understanding and appreciation of life, taught me patience and above all the power of love.